Oasis in the Desert

By Cyantha Hookey
From Doomadgee Community,
Queensland

Library For All Ltd.

Library For All is an Australian not for profit organisation with a mission to make knowledge accessible to all via an innovative digital library solution. Visit us at libraryforall.org

Oasis in the Desert

First published 2023

Published by Library For All Ltd
Email: info@libraryforall.org
URL: libraryforall.org

Library For All gratefully acknowledges the contributions of all who made previous editions of this book possible.

This edition made possible by the generous contributions of GSK and 54 reasons.

Our Yarning logo design by Jason Lee, Bidjipidji Art

Original illustrations by Fariza Dzatalin Nurtsani

Oasis in the Desert
Hookey, Cyantha
ISBN: 978-1-923110-34-2
SKU03358

Oasis in the Desert

We respect and honour Aboriginal and Torres Strait Islander Elders past, present and future. We acknowledge the stories, traditions and living cultures of Aboriginal and Torres Strait Islander peoples on this land and commit to building a brighter future together.

Adels Grove, in Waanyi Country (Far North Queensland), is known by the name *Wududaji* — meaning *lizard* in Waanyi language.

It is called an "Oasis in the Desert" because of the beautiful, mesmerising clear flowing stream water that never runs dry.

Close by is Boodjumulla National Park, where you can go on the canoes, take a cruise, or walk up the gorge.

It takes two hours following the backroad from Doomadgee to get to Adels Grove.

When families are taken there for a weekend, and they see how beautiful the scenery is, they all say, "Wow!"

Splash!

"Look, I can see a turtle!"

"Look, one big bream there too!"

"Can we go for a swim once we reach the gorge?"

"Yeah okay. We'll go swimming at the end of the cruise trip."

After swimming at the national park, we go back to Adels Grove.

We do the other activities with the ladies.

Afterwards, we go fishing.

The next day, the families have more fun choices.

"You can stay at the grove to go swimming with the kids or you can go fishing for *wabinbarra* (turtle) and *kaku* (fish)."

Back at camp, we paint, make damper, write stories, and rest up for the evening.

We make a campfire to cook our catch and have a feast of bush tucker.

And we yarn to each other about our day.

Sitting around the campfire, we yarn about how fat the turtle and fish were, and how we loved going on the boat ride up to the gorge.

The kids always say how cold the water is when they are swimming, but it still never stops them!

Tomorrow, we will drive back to Doomadgee.

On the trip home, the families can't stop talking about how good their weekend away on Waanyi Country was and how they are going to come back.

You can use these questions to talk about this book with your family, friends and teachers.

What did you learn from this book?

Describe this book in one word. Funny? Scary? Colourful? Interesting?

How did this book make you feel when you finished reading it?

What was your favourite part of this book?

download our reader app
getlibraryforall.org

Hello Readers!

In 2021, Save The Children Australia and Library For All worked with the Doomadgee community to develop a children's book series. The stories were written in English and translated into Gangalidda, Garrawa and Waanyi, three of the most widely spoken languages in the region. Beautiful illustrations and engaging photos were selected to ensure these books encourage children to learn to read, and love to read, while celebrating culture and country.

Our Yarning

Want to discover more books from this collection? Our Yarning is a collection of books written by Aboriginal and Torres Strait Islander peoples across Australia.

We know that children learn better, and enjoy reading more, when they see themselves in the stories, characters and illustrations of the books they read.

To download the app, visit the Google Play Store on any Android device and search 'Our Yarning'.

librariforall.org

www.ingramcontent.com/pod-product-compliance
Lightning Source LLC
Chambersburg PA
CBHW040122070426
42448CB00042B/3447